A JOURNEY TO T

OF ADVENT

MW01612568

First Print Edition: November 2014

Contents

Introduction

Purpose

Christmas is coming.

Those three words strike fear into many hearts. Not because winter comes with it. Even if the temperatures were exactly what we all needed, with snow where it is needed and none where it's not, Christmas still scares us.

Why?

Perhaps we would do well to define what Christmas is, because fear grows from uncertainty. What is Christmas? For many of us, Christmas is too many things at once. It is a religious observance, a cultural celebration, a family event, and a work nightmare. It's a school break and a vacation time. Christmas ends up being too much at once.

For our own sakes, we need to trim Christmas down a bit. This book will not take down the Christmas trees that have been up in Wal-Mart for a month already, nor will it make it easier to be three places at the same time with your family this December. I cannot solve in these few pages all the divergent ways Christian churches celebrate the holiday and sort out the cultural confusion of a Christian holiday in a country that wants it celebrated without mentioning Jesus. At least, only bring Him up of there's a profit in it.

Let us evaluate what we are celebrating. There will be some references to the general commercial culture we live in America, but the focus is on the religious observance of Christmas. Specifically, on the Christian religious observance. My assumption is that you have picked up an Advent-oriented devotional book because you want to find space in your Christmas observance to focus on Jesus.

That's what this book is for: to help with the focus on

Jesus. In the interest of that, let me disclose a few foundations for you.

First, I am a Christian. This is not a look at Christmas from a skeptical viewpoint. I believe that Jesus was born of a virgin, lived a sinless life, died in place of sinners, and rose up from the grave on the third day. I hold these views fully and they form the foundation for the rest of this discussion. It's not possible for me look beyond these, for I find that life itself builds from this foundation.

Second, I am a sola scriptura type of Christian. I firmly believe that everything we <u>need</u> for Christian faith is in Scripture. Obviously, I think we can find help in other places, or I wouldn't write this. I'd just copy and paste text from Scripture. Anything else though, be it good traditions or great opinions or personal deep feelings, comes secondary to Scripture as the rule of faith. This even includes human-developed definitions and explanations. I hold that Scripture is God-breathed and useful (2 Timothy 3:16), and that human terms like infallible and inerrant[1] are good explanations of that idea.

Third, I am a sola fide/sola gratia type of Christian. Salvation is by grace through faith, not by any

---

[1] These two terms mean slightly different things. Infallible typically is taken as meaning "always right about matters of faith" while Inerrant is taken as meaning "containing no errors on anything."

I am not convinced that Scripture has any errors--as being God-breathed, God makes no errors. However, I also see that His process of delivering Scripture has left us with challenges like textual issues that may soften how dogmatic we can be about minor details. The case of the height of Goliath is a good example. Is he four cubits and a span or cubits and a span? Is the Masoretic Text the right one or the Dead Sea Scrolls? Some of our "inerrancy" stances don't handle that well.

works nor by your membership in the right Christian organization. Christians who are obeying God seek fellowship with other Christians for worship, encouragement, growth, and service. That fellowship becomes a church.[2] Church participation follows faith, but does not save from sin. Only Jesus saves us from our sin.

Finally, I am a solus Christus type of Christian. I believe that there is one mediator between God and humanity, and that is Jesus of Nazareth. To be unpopular about it, there is right belief and wrong belief, and Christian belief is right.

These are my foundational points. Like a good building, there are walls that build up on these foundations. If we were digging into theology, we would go there next. We're not. We are going towards Christmas through the

---

[2] Just because a place calls itself a church doesn't make it one, nor does lacking the label make a place not a church.

Advent season, so let's deal with that by previewing what we will and will not accomplish here.

This book will:

1. Take a daily look at parts of the Christmas story

2. Look at the common and less common parts of the Christmas story

3. Help you look at the implications of the coming of Jesus on your life

This book will not:

1. Answer the debate about whether or not Jesus was born in December, March, or September. That's an intriguing debate, but one for the academic side.

2. Wrestle deeply with the idea that we should take no notice of Christmas at all. I will suggest to you why I think it's of value to go ahead and take note of Christmas, but if you are convinced it is a bad idea to observe a day as

differently important for Christian life, I am surprised you've read this far.

3. Finish your Christmas shopping for you. It will, however, help you get a head start on next year's because you can buy copies for everyone!

With those stated aims, here is why I find value in observing the Advent Season:

Habits are hard to form. It's that simple. Habits of walking plainly and openly with Christ in a chaotic world are not easily formed in our hearts and lives. Taking the time out of one of the busier seasons of life actually forms a habit that becomes easier to carry over into the rest of the year.

Faith on display shows integrity this time of year. I understand not wanting to "piggy-back" your faith onto everything else right now. Like you, I'm not sure if anything is more annoying than that guy on Facebook who throws Christian rebuttals at every mention of Santa, reindeer, and stockings. But for us as Christians to keep silent now while the world talks about Christ is not just lazy, it is dishonest. Are we going to keep our faith silent as if we have none? While the wider world sings of Jesus, we're going to ignore Him? That seems wrong on many levels.

The madness has to stop somewhere. Let it stop here. You feel it. You've felt it since the Christmas decorations went up in October as the "End of Summer" clearance sales wrapped up. It's too much. You know it. I know it. Let us work together to do something about it.

How to use this book

This book has a simple format. There are entries for each Sunday of Advent. Then, there are five entries for each week. That gives the freedom to miss a day or to focus on something else at least once a week. Each entry will have a few questions to spur discussion and one recommended hymn or song for that day. If you cannot bring yourself to sing or if you are not familiar with the tune, try to look for it on YouTube. If I have a specific version to commend, I will put a link in the footnotes.

An important note is that this book is undated. Advent is a calendar-based event, starting four Sundays before Christmas. It has a different starting point each year, and a different length each year. For example, Advent starts November 30 in 2014, but November 29 in 2015. In 2017 Advent will begin December 3!

With that in mind, I offer you a full four weeks of devotionals, knowing that some years that might be too many. Feel free to read extra when the Advent season is short, but there won't be a test, so don't worry about it.

I want to establish one thing plainly based on that statement: you cannot fail at observing Advent. If you do nothing more than move thirty seconds of your day from self-centered to Christ-centered, you have made progress. I do not hope to instill a sense of legalism about your Christmas season, nor do I wish you to see me as, or become yourself, a Christmas Pharisee who demands conformity.

The Christian faith, while dealing with individual spiritual needs, is lived out in community with other believers. I encourage you to walk with others to the manger of Jesus and behold the newborn King.

Also, allow me to suggest a few albums for a Christmas soundtrack. Most of these are available on CD and digitally and are worth your investment.

How Many Kings: Songs for Christmas by downhere

Noel by Josh Wilson

A Family Christmas by The Piano Guys

Have a Merry Little Christmas Darling EP by Sarah Darling

Joy-An Irish Christmas by Keith and Kristyn Getty

The Hymns and Carols of Christmas by Jim Brickman

Appreciation

First of all, one does not celebrate the Advent of Jesus without thinking of Jesus. What would we have to celebrate if we were still in our sins? Not a thing.

Second of all, Proverbs tells us that he who finds a wife finds a good thing. My beloved wife, Ann, has held my feet to the fire to do this again after I took a shot at this a few years ago.

Third of all, I am blessed to serve a church that not only tolerates but encourages my pipe dreams like writing.

Finally, to those of you who read the first Advent Reflections in 2011 and did not tell me to quit writing, thank you.

Week One

Sunday: In Bethlehem

While they were there, the days were completed for her to give birth. (Luke 2:6 NASB)

Where should we begin this year's Advent observances? That is a question I have wrestled with while preparing these short devotionals. In a prior effort, I examined the gifts of Christmas (gold, frankincense, and myrrh) to look at the meaning of Christmas. This year, I want to look at the places of Christmas. Where does the story happen? There are many that matter to the story. Consider the Garden of Eden and the plains of Canaan. Think 0f Egypt, or Midian, or Jericho. Imagine the hills of Bethlehem, walked by a shepherd boy with a slingshot. Contrast those hills with the halls of Babylon, walked by the prophet Daniel, or the halls of Jerusalem, walked by Isaiah and Jeremiah and Micah. Add to those the Temple of Solomon, the Temple of Haggai, the Temple of Herod...and the village of Nazareth. We even see the curtain pulled back and see how all the heavens touch Christmas.

Where to start?

I am not the wisest of teachers born of men, but I know that the Great Teacher wrote the story in the first place. And where did He start? He started in Bethlehem. He did not start out there on the hills with the sheep or in the city gates of governance.

He started in a manger, just outside an inn. He started when her days were completed and the Incarnation became visible to everyone. We will, therefore, start there. That manger held the Son of God, born for the salvation of mankind. Christmas celebrates that moment, and we will do well to start looking toward Christmas Day from that point.

After all, we face the Advent season with this great blessing: we know the whole story. We are not seeing the story unfold in the first place, as Mary and Joseph did, nor are we jumping in later with the Apostles. We are blessed to look back and know how it ends. We know the terrible glory that is the Cross, the amazing glory that is the Resurrection, and the astonishing glory that is the Ascension.

So we look back, starting at the manger. We remember that Christ was born. Born of a virgin named Mary, chosen by God in His grace--for Scripture gives us no compelling details of her that would pick her. Born to the family of a carpenter, a construction man, named Joseph, who enters quietly stage left, stays for a few years, and departs with no definitive word of when he left. Two people who are highly ordinary, except for the work of God in their lives.

They come to a highly ordinary place called Bethlehem.

True, it is the City of David, but under Roman domination, what does that mean? Precious little. After all,

Judea is over near the edge of the empire and hardly that big of a deal. The Romans trade with their territory in Egypt via ship, so the old need for land trade through Israel has abated.

Christmas, then, comes when Someone beyond extraordinary comes into this world through an almost boringly ordinary story: born in Bethlehem, in a manger, because of government bureaucracy. Born on time, at the completion of her days, so that His days could begin.

Let us begin, then, to see how our ordinary lives are transformed as we learn of and walk with the Extraordinary One.

His name is Jesus.

Have you ever felt too ordinary to be of use? Do you think that God can still do extraordinary things through ordinary places?

Hymn for the Day: "O Little Town of Bethlehem" by Phillips Brooks. (#196 in the *2008 Baptist Hymnal* from Lifeway Worship.)

Special Music for the Week: "Child of Bethlehem" by Wayne Watson (on his 1994 Album *One Christmas Eve*, also available digitally)

Day 1: Before Creation

In the beginning was the Word, and the Word was with God, and the Word was God. (John 1:1 NASB)

We go backwards from Bethlehem to a place that is hard to define. Somewhere, outside of our ability to judge time, is a time and a place where creation was not. A time and a place when there were no stars, no comets, no asteroids. There were no clouds of dust or life forms anywhere. There was, for all we can measure looking back, nothing.

Nothing, except for God. This is the message we move to next, though we cannot rightly place where it occurs on the map. As Biblical Christians, we believe that God is everywhere while also acknowledging that He is beyond everywhere. Creation does not contain Him or limit Him, yet He permeates what He has made.

So we look back and see that before the world was made, the Word was. And He was with God and was God. This idea defies simplistic explanation, but it is beautiful for faithful understanding. God is both One and Three, what is termed the Trinity. We see that God the Father and God the Son, Jesus, exist in the very beginning. We see later that the Holy Spirit, the Third Person of the Trinity, exists in the same time, but He is not so much in view here.

What does this tell us? What do we gather from the presence of Jesus all the way back at the beginning?

We learn this: Christmas was but a moment in His life. It was the beginning of His life as the Incarnate Word, where He took on flesh and emptied Himself. Yet He always was before then. Through the goods and the bads of eternity, He was and is and will be.

For us, this holds an important reminder. Christmas comes as a reminder of a moment, but Christ came as One who is eternal. Every year, we see the advertising begin to roll around about making the holidays better than ever or about not spoiling the season.

We see the hints in the TV programs and movies that we watch warning us about the demise of Christmas because of some slighted portion of a contract or a missed bus connection. Those films and funnies have their place in entertainment, and some of them are quite high on my all-time favorites list.

Yet we need to keep in mind that nothing we can do will stop Christmas from coming, nor does Advent rely on our knowing how to keep it in our hearts, whether anyone knows how. Instead, our dependence is on the Eternal One who chose to step from an unmeasured reality down into time and space. Our celebration of the season should begin with thinking about the immense distance covered for Christmas. Not the lengths we go to the mall or the miles covered by the one in the brown suit (the UPS driver) who brings the gifts. The lengths God took to being here with us, among us.

We cannot stop Christmas because the whole of eternity is pouring in to that one moment in history. Instead, let us celebrate Christ by beginning our season committed to resting in Him through it all.

What are some ways that you can practice resting in the knowledge the Christmas is God's work, not yours? How does knowing God is eternal help you pace your life in all things?

Hymn for the Day: "Ancient Words" by Lynn DeShazo. (#344 in the *2008 Baptist Hymnal* from Lifeway Worship.)

Day 2: Out of the Garden

I will put enmity between you and the woman,

And between your offspring and her offspring;

He shall bruise your head,

And you shall bruise his heel. (Genesis 3:15

ESV)

We go from unmeasurable eternity to definite, but

lost, reality. Our maps cannot pin down where the Garden of

Eden once was, though Genesis describes the rivers that

flowed around it. If we were exploring Genesis, I would

suggest that one effect of the flood of Genesis 6 was the

elimination of all remaining traces of the Garden, an

irreparable breach with the place of our ancestors. However,

this is not that book, so we will move on.

The Garden was a great place. God Himself said so,

which is not something He says of many other places in

Scripture. Even in that good place, though, there was

trouble. There were people. These were people, though, with no prior problems. No history of slip-ups and fall downs. They had no history at all! Yet, even in that very good place, temptation came, and Adam and Eve fell. They chose to reject God's instructions for life and His singular command to avoid death--and brought death upon us all.

That, more than anything else, made the world we live in. The modern political climate is not to blame. Nor the change in climate, nor any other measurable issue. The introduction of willful sin into the Creation of God alone is to blame. It brought a darkness, a sundering of the connection between God and humanity that the world is not capable of compensating for. Coming to the Garden of Eden is, unfortunately, a sad arrival for us as we make our way back to the manger. The Garden is the picture of what should have been and is not.

Perhaps you see your life in the Garden. You can easily list all the should-have-beens, all the wish-I-hads of your days. The list of single decisions, or worse, the chain of decisions, that have brought you to today weigh so heavily on you that Marley looks at ease in comparison. What can you do, then? The cords of death seem to entangle all that you do. You cannot see the light, much less run freely into it. Christmas is, in truth, a time to see yourself another year deeper, not in debt, but in the mire.

You are in the right place, then. You are right where the Christmas story hits the timeline of human history, because you are just outside the Garden. You see where we are and grasp the results of serpents afflicting us with every little step. Yet that serpent is not victorious--far from it!

See the promise in Genesis 3:15? Enmity between the serpent and the woman; a promise of destruction. For a bruised head is an irrevocable wound! Standing there outside the Garden, seeing the wasteland brought about by sin, Adam and Eve were in the same place we often are: in need of hope. God gave it to them in this, the first promise of the coming of Jesus. Advent begins on the calendar four Sundays before Christmas Day, but Advent in our life begins the moment we look up from the chaos and recognize God's grace and His promises for our life. And not for our life only, but for the lives of all those around us.

If you could undo one decision in your life, what would it be? How can you use that thought to change your perspective on life now? How has God used the results of that decision in your life? Are you willing to let Him transform your life through that?

Hymn for the Day: "Come, Thou Long-Expected Jesus" by Charles Wesley. (#176 in the *2008 Baptist Hymnal* by Lifeway Worship.)

Day 3: In Early Rome

Then there will be a fourth kingdom as strong as iron; inasmuch as iron crushes and shatters all things, so, like iron that breaks in pieces, it will crush and break all these in pieces. (Daniel 2:40 NASB)

Our next stop on the way to the Manger is a hill, quite some distance from Bethlehem. Actually, we see a group of seven hills come into focus as we arrive, for we have come to Rome. Why is Rome important to the Christmas story? Let us explore the reasons that Rome factors into the places that matter this Advent.

First, Rome was the seat of power that ruled over the land of Israel at that time. Rome was so dominant that, had Jesus been given a government birth certificate, it would have placed His birth year around 749 AUC, or ab urbe condita, the number of years since the founding of Rome. Not only did all roads lead to Rome, as the proverb says, but the calendar ran as if there was no time before Rome. Roman culture may not have been beloved of Israelites, but it was ever present in their lives.

Second, Rome was in an era of expansion and growth at the time of the first Christmas. We know this because the Roman Empire was expanding and growing for most of its initial existence. Without becoming a Roman history text here, I would suggest that Rome expands until Nero and Caligula start the process of wasting the empire on their own decadence. These both came to power after the birth of Christ, though, so under Augustus Caesar we see Rome still expanding. Because of her expansion, the city needs a clear tax and draft record. Therefore, a decree goes out which moves Joseph and Mary to Bethlehem.

Third, Rome was foreseen as the last great human empire. Our Scripture passage speaks to this, as Daniel provides God's interpretation of Nebuchadnezzar's dream. Nebuchadnezzar saw a kingdom initially of iron and saw that kingdom grow and intermingle with others, eventually falling. But in the days of that kingdom, God set up a kingdom which will never be destroyed, a kingdom that fills the earth. Rome matters to Christmas because it was in the time of this great kingdom that God had promised to establish His kingdom on earth.

His kingdom will have no end. Even more, His kingdom exceeds all the kingdoms before it and endures beyond all kingdoms after it.

There is something truly amazing about this. In Daniel 2, we follow along as Daniel speaks to Nebuchadnezzar about Rome in the sixth century before Christ. At this time, Rome had yet to become the dominant city in Italy, much less create an empire. The Republic of Rome was 200 years away, although during this era legend tells us that the king of Rome added the family Octavia to the Senate. The Octavii would, in due time, see Gaius Octavius adopted by Julius and titled Augustus by the Roman Senate, ending the republic and marking the beginning of the empire.

The Advent of Jesus was prepared for many centuries before Mary and Joseph sought an inn, even before many of the leaders of Israel knew that He would come. At the time of Daniel's prophecy, the Israelites were mourning the destruction of the Temple and their deportation to Babylon and wondering what hope the future held.

It held Jesus, the promise of Him shared not only with Israel but also with pagan Babylon. It was worked out through Rome.

Does your life feel overrun with sadness right now? Or perhaps like there are too many great kingdoms causing you difficulty? Is it possible that God is working out a long-term plan for you? What would you like it to be? Are you willing to let it be something other than what you have planned?

Hymn for the Day: "Joy Has Dawned<u>"</u> by Keith Getty and Stuart Townsend (#186 in the *2008 Baptist Hymnal* by Lifeway Worship)

Day 4: Under the Stars

And He took him (Abram) outside and said, "Now look toward the heavens, and count the stars, if you are able to count them." And He said to him, "So shall your descendants be." (Genesis 15:5 NASB)

We come now to the hills of Canaan, though we know not exactly where. Abram is recorded in the preceding chapter as dwelling by the oaks of Mamre, but no one thought to put up a sign on the right tree for us. This is part of our extended challenge in studying the events of Scripture: modern people go ahead put up plaques and mark GPS coordinates of important events. Ancient people were less committed to leaving markers for future historians.

Wherever Abram specifically was, though, is not as important as the events that transpire in Genesis 15. Abram has famously left his father's people and his home country and gone where God guided him, as he was commanded in

Genesis 12. The road so far has not been easy, though, and Abram is getting old. He took his nephew with him, perhaps in hopes his nephew would be his heir. Family squabbles led to the sundering of that relationship, though Abram went to great lengths to save Lot from captivity in Genesis 14. After the rescue, Abram found himself alone again. His integrity refused a relationship with the wicked kings that he rescued alongside Lot. Then Lot returned with the kings rather than returning to Abram.

There are few ways to be more alone than to live among many people and have no good relationships with any of them. Abram despairs at this point, doubting God's ability to bring the promise of a new nation to fulfillment. Abram has no clear picture of how he will even have a family to survive him, and he sees bleakness in the future.

Yet God is not limited by the imagination of man. Whatever it is that we think God can do, we find that He is able to do much more than this. So, God sends Abram out to look at the stars. He would have seen even more stars than most of you see, because I can assure you that light pollution was not a problem on the hills of Canaan! Each of those stars reminded Abram of a world bigger and greater than he fully understood, and the immeasurable vastness of space pointed him to the God who had created it all.

Abram trusted God here and believed that he would have an heir. He even believed that his children would become a great nation. What Abram most likely did not grasp was this: the Promise of God was not solely focused on biology. Instead, the promise given on those hills looked forward to something even greater than one great nation.

The promise anticipated the Kingdom of God, made up of every tribe and tongue and people, all united through Jesus. This is the great glory of the promise under the stars: God will not be limited by anything man can see or plan.

How much chaos do you have this week? How

many ways have your plans and expectations failed? If you could imagine the perfect solution, what would it be? Can you come to the point this Christmas of realizing that your best will pale in comparison to God's actions?

Hymn for the Day: "To God Be the Glory" by Fanny J. Crosby (#28 in the *2008 Baptist Hymnal* from Lifeway Christian Resources)

Day 5: On the Road to the Laundry

Therefore the Lord Himself will give you a sign:
Behold, a virgin will be with child and bear a son, and she
will call His name Immanuel. (Isaiah 7:14, NASB)

Now we come to the roads of Jerusalem, quite
literally on the way to the ancient equivalent of the
laundromat. Isaiah has gone to meet King Ahaz. This was
not a pleasant meeting, as the people were terrified of
imminent invasion. The Arameans had camped out in the
hill country of Ephraim, and the unified armies of Ephraim
and Aram were preparing to invade the nation of Judah.
Their eyes were set on Jerusalem, and the numbers were in
the invaders' favor.

In the midst of this, Isaiah is sent to King Ahaz to
carry a message of hope. But he is not sent alone. He takes
his son, Shear-Jashub, and they meet the king. God speaks
through Isaiah, commanding that Ahaz and the people not be

afraid, that they be calm, and that they trust in the salvation of God. God then offers Ahaz what so many people long for: a sign. God tells him to ask for a sign--no matter how complex or bizarre, how deep or how high. Ahaz responds with a mock piety, saying that he will not test God, forgetting that disobedience is not a sign of belief. God then promises a sign, one that has been a stumbling block for many across the centuries.

God promises a Child. Not just any child, but a Child born of a virgin. The promise Isaiah shares with Ahaz raises a debate, because the Hebrew word for "virgin" can also mean "young woman." The explanation is this: the prophecy held a dual fulfillment utilizing both meanings. The first was immediate. A young woman in Isaiah's day was able to marry and have a child even in the time of fear. And by the time the son was old enough to know good from bad, the threatening kings were gone--their kingdom destroyed. This was a sure reminder to the people of Israel that God was with them, making the child a sign rightly called Immanuel.

Yet several centuries later, the Spirit inspires Matthew to explain the second and greater fulfillment of Isaiah's words. Matthew quotes Isaiah, using the Greek word not for young woman, but for virgin. Matthew tells us that the fullness of the promised sign of Immanuel was not simply God's deliverance of one people at one time, but God's deliverance of all people for all time. Immanuel was born, not of a young woman brave enough to marry in time of war, but of a virgin, brave enough to trust God in all things.

So our place today is on the road to the laundry field, where God promises something amazing. He promises that, even in the midst of war and chaos, He is with us. Not only is He with us, though, He is willing to show us that reality. There are many promises of God that hinge on taking His word for it, but His presence and His redemption are not those promises. He is with us to show us these things by showing us Himself in Jesus, Immanuel.

Have you ever longed for a sign from God? Is the sign you would like any greater than realizing that He came down and dwelt with us? Does it strengthen your faith to consider Christmas as the great sign of God's love and presence?

Hymn for the Day: "O Come, O Come, Emmanuel" (#175 in the *2008 Baptist Hymnal* by Lifeway Worship)

Week 2

Sunday: Down in Egypt

God saw the people of Israel--and God knew. (Exodus 2:23 ESV)

Suffering. Oppression. Genocide, by action or inaction.

All of these can be found in the world today. These societal problems are hardly the type of thing we like to think about during Christmas, though. As we enjoy the blessings of liberty and prosperity, troubles around the world are easy to ignore.

It is not so easy for the all-knowing God to ignore anything. Let us turn to this week's beginning place: the land of Egypt. Egypt is a constant feature in the narratives of the Bible, involved in every phase of history. Abraham traveled there, and it is an Egyptian ship that Paul boards for the last stage of his journey to Rome in Acts 28.

Egypt is the central location of the second book of the Bible, Exodus, which is where we are today. For background, it is worth noting that the people of Israel here have not yet become a nation. They are the descendants of Jacob, son of Isaac, son of Abraham. Some four centuries prior to our passage, the small family had traveled to Egypt to reunite with one brother and to survive the famine plaguing the Mediterranean world of the time.

Now the Israelites are numerous. Pharaoh has decided to reduce their numbers and oppress them, for reasons of state. At this point, the Israelites experience the suffering, oppression, and genocide that still plague differing peoples today. They cry out; they groan for relief.

And God knew. He heard. He raised up a deliverer, a man named Moses. Moses leads the people from oppression to freedom, a journey of many years. God works through

Moses, and a nation is born.

The people of Israel are not the only ones to know suffering, oppression, and genocide. We see these throughout history, around the world, and no society is immune to them. These are part of our heritage as people with a sinful nature. It is a heritage that we need deliverance from. But unlike the Exodus, this journey is not one that finishes.

Why?

Because there is always a new generation needing deliverance. There is a need for one greater than Moses. One who is eternal and able to go back, every day, to the suffering and bring them out. God knows our everlasting need for a deliverer, and gave us One who is everlasting. He gave Himself.

From this, we should take two major actions this Advent season. First, worship with our whole hearts. Not because we are compelled by command, but because we are driven by deliverance. There is nothing better than being free; freedom should bring praise to our lips.

Second, we should find and fulfill small actions that follow in the Savior's footsteps. He has left us with two major tasks: proclaim freedom from sin, and enable freedom from suffering. We should seek out those who face suffering, oppression, or genocide and do all within our power to deliver them. It is a business that God has been in for many years, and one in which we may participate wherever we are.

What is one way you can help others who are suffering this week? Are there ways to invest your life in delivering others through proclaiming the Gospel and relieving the ailments of humanity?

Hymn for the day: "Come, Thou Long Expected

Jesus" by Charles Wesley (#176 in the *2008 Baptist Hymnal*

by Lifeway Worship)

Special music for the week: "Rejoice at Christmas" by

Andrew Wight, recorded by Sarah Darling. (Available

digitally at Amazon or iTunes. YouTube link:

https://www.youtube.com/watch?v=aJz9ZkfyM58)

Day 1: Around the Mountain

Now when all the people saw the thunder and the flashes of lightning and the sound of the trumpet and the mountain smoking, the people were afraid and trembled, and they stood far off and said to Moses, "You speak to us, and we will listen; but do not let God speak to us, lest we die." Moses said to the people, "Do not fear, for God has come to test you, that the fear of him may be before you, that you may not sin." The people stood far off, while Moses drew near to the thick darkness where God was. (Exodus 20:18–21, ESV)

Gathered at the mountain, the people of Israel see God come down in fire and thunder. They hear His voice from the midst of the cloud.

And they are afraid. God presents them with the basics of the covenant, what we recall as the Ten commandments, and speaks to the people. Their fear, though, drives them away. Our passage shows us how they stand far away, rejecting God and the intimacy He offers them. A representative can come and speak to God first and then go back to the people, but they refuse to go to God directly. If they draw near to God themselves, they reason, death will result.

This fear is very human. It was Adam and Eve's initial response to sin, for it explains the shame they felt at their nakedness. We ,too, carry a deep-seated fear of intimacy with God. It is not a phobia, though, nor is it an irrational fear. All things considered, we are more foolish to think we can hide from the Almighty at all than we are to be afraid of His presence.

So what do the people around the mountain have to do with the people around the manger? As we consider Christmas, a few contrasts are in order. First, the plain around the mountain was open. The manger? A closed-in space. Second, the appearance of God at the mountain was a fraction of His glory and power. Yet at the manger, we see God come down as a little baby. The most fragile form that humanity can take.

Why does this matter?

It matters because God is coming to us, in our fear, in our helplessness. He knows that we not only cannot approach Him, but that we also will not. In grace and mercy, then, God comes to us. He does not come as He did at Sinai, but He comes as one who is approachable. He does not remove His holiness and power in doing so, but He veils them.

Our God is approachable, relatable. Not because we have made Him so, but because that is His choice. The various encounters with God throughout Scripture, from around the mountain to the manger, each teach a point about Him. And the point of Christmas is that we need not fear to look upon the Lord and to hear Him speak. He speaks with grace; He speaks with mercy.

Does this mean we are wrong to expect death? Nonsense. Death is the result of sin coming into the presence of God, for God cannot permit sin. That death was taken by Jesus at the Cross, though, and for those who will approach and accept the grace of God, there is no need to fear the intimacy of God any longer. We share in His death, so that we may share in His life.

As the world stands now, though, the question is this: will we react as if we are around the mountain? Or around the manger?

What are some ways you can practice the intimacy of God? What parts of your life might He put to death so that you can share in His life?

Hymn for the Day: "O Come, All Ye Faithful" by John Francis Wade (#199 in the *2008 Baptist Hymnal*).

Day 2: Over in Moab

So Boaz took Ruth, and she became his wife. And he went in to her, and the LORD gave her conception, and she bore a son. (Ruth 4:13 ESV)

Ruth has her own book of the Bible, one you would do well to read. From that book, we see that she is from the land of Moab. Moab was a neighboring country to Israel, and the two did not get along very well. For details on the national relationships, take a look at Genesis 19, Numbers 22, Judges 3, and 2 Kings 3. If you take the time to read those, you'll realize that the two groups just did not get along.

Yet we find Ruth, a Moabite woman, holding not only her own book of Scripture but appearing in the genealogy of Jesus Himself in Matthew 1:5. Her story is more like ours than many of us would care to admit. She comes from a nation condemned for its sins. She comes from a family that has seen more than its share of heartache. First, her father-in-law abandoned his homeland. Then her parents married her off to that family of foreigners. Few commentaries I have deal with this, but ancient cultures were fairly unwilling to marry their children to foreigners. Ruth's family giving her in marriage to an Israelite sojourner family suggests that either the Moabites held her in disregard or Elimelech had gained wealth enough to be worth holding on to.

Either way, considering the typical culture of the time, Ruth was hardly afforded any respect in this situation. She was treated as disposable by her family and her culture. Once Mahlon, her husband, died, her people did not want her back. Even as she traveled back to Israel with her mother-in-law, she met one more rejection as Orpah left the family and returned home.

There is so much heartbreak in the story of Naomi and

Ruth, one exults in the happy ending of the short story. Ruth finds a new husband, who does not leave her penniless and hopeless, and Naomi is blessed. This is not, in itself, all that remarkable. All great love stories overcome hardships (or, in my case, a hard head). Not all great love stories result in the Messiah coming from their line. In fact, any love story has to fit somewhere among the names in Matthew 1 or Luke 3 to accomplish that.

Ruth's does, teaching us that even over in Moab, God was at work. In all the situations that Ruth faced, the tragic and the excellent, God had His sovereign plan at work. Ruth could not see it then, but she lived out her part with enduring faith.

You may be in Moab right now. Perhaps you feel rejected and lost, or you have traveled far and wide because of a famine in your land. Whatever the case may be, as you step another day closer to the manger, consider this:

Famine and rejection, exile and poverty, love and life

all lead to the day when Christ comes. Celebrating Him does not require the bad things to never have happened. Instead, let Him redeem you and the good things will be even better.

Have you ever experienced tragedy or rejection? Can you find others who have suffered as well to mutually strengthen this year? Can your hope in Christ overshadow your heartbreak?

Hymn for the day: "Joy to the World" by Isaac Watts (# in the *2008 Baptist Hymnal* by Lifeway Worship)

Day 3: Away from Shiloh

And she called the boy Ichabod, saying, "The glory has departed from Israel," because the ark of God was taken and because of her father-in-law and her husband. She said, "The glory has departed from Israel, for the ark of God was taken." (1 Samuel 4:21–22 NASB)

We come to one of the darker points on our tour of places leading to the manger. We sit on the outskirts of a town called Shiloh. This is the place where the tabernacle of God, made during the Exodus as the center of worship, has come to rest. Further, here is the center of Israelite worship. It is the place where the ark of the covenant was kept.

WAS kept, because the Israelites had carried this symbol of God's presence and promise into their battle with the Philistines. The Israelites had done so haphazardly, going to war with a symbol of God and not the approval of

God. They lost both the battle and the ark. Word returns quickly to Shiloh of the defeat, for the treasures of Israel are held there. The Philistines are coming.

When that occurs, a baby boy is born. Phinehas, one of the priests, had gone to the battle to carry the ark. He was killed, leaving a pregnant widow. As she heard the news of her husband, brother-in-law, and father-in-law perishing along with the army of Israel, labor set in. She passes in childbirth, naming her son Ichabod as she dies. Why Ichabod? It means "no glory," basically, and is a lament. She sees that God's glory has departed Israel, and fears for what this child will face living in a land without God.

It's a terrible name. He will go through life as a reminder of the bad times, assuming that he gets to go through life at all. Remember that the enemies of Israel are coming to plunder and kill. This child is named to represent all the fears and concerns that his mother had.

What does that have do with us?

We carry the circumstances of life with us, including where and how we were born. Ichabod could be any of us, born without hope. Born into a world of disease and warfare, there appears little hope. We see a world around us which screams for Christmas to be called off, for there is no hope to be had!

Yet we come to the manger and find another baby. His name was chosen, just as Ichabod's name was. His is "Jesus," and likely in his native language more of "Yeshua." What does this name mean?

"Deliverer." Or, perhaps, "Savior." It carries the idea of being the response to a cry of need, a cry that is answered by the God of the covenant.

Ichabod may be your family name. It may be the name you have given yourself or your people while you run away from Shiloh, fearing for your future.

There is a greater name. It is not one that we may claim for ourselves, but instead is the One who was given for us. You may have been born Ichabod, but He was born Jesus and His glory will exceed your needs and hopes.

What problems do you think you cannot overcome? Does God provide guidance about these in His word? Is there any sin in your life that is greater than Jesus' forgiveness?

Hymn for the Day: "What Child is This?" by William C. Dix. (#198 in the *2008 Baptist Hymnal* from Lifeway Worship.)

Day 4: Back in Bethlehem

Now the LORD said to Samuel, "How long will you grieve over Saul, since I have rejected him from being king over Israel? Fill your horn with oil and go; I will send you to Jesse the Bethlehemite, for I have selected a king for Myself among his sons."(1 Samuel 16:1 NASB)

We come back to Bethlehem, about 1000 BC. (That's a rough date, not a precise one.) Saul sits on the throne of Israel. The people serve Saul, even though his disobedience has brought God's judgment on him as king. Samuel the prophet knows that God has rejected Saul. He knows because God sent Samuel to tell Saul!

Samuel grieves for Saul. He grieves for the nation of Israel. Samuel saw the people demand a king and warned them that it was not a good idea. They wanted one anyway, and God granted their request with the cautions that the king would take more than he should and would take what was rightly God's. The people got their king, and he promptly turned out to be a military hero. Then he truly fulfilled the people's wish: they had longed for a king just like the nations around them. The nations rejected Israel's God. So did Saul.

Samuel remains the voice of the Lord God for Israel. Yet he grieves over what he percieves to be the inevitable decline of his nation. He grieves like one who has no hope. And God will have him stop it. How?

God sends Samuel to Bethlehem. Up until now, Bethlehem has not been a major city in Israel. When it has shown up, the mentions are unhappy. From Jacob's burial of his beloved Rachel to the Levite of Judges 17, Bethlehem is associated with death.

Bethlehem needs a better reputation. Ruth's story unfolded in Bethlehem, and her story depicted the redemption not only of an individual but of a town. What is a town, after all, but a group of people striving through life together? So the reader of Scripture now sees Bethlehem as a place of hope and not despair.

Samuel, however, does not yet see the hope. God sends him there just the same. He goes, fearing the response of the king. He arrives, and the city elders fear the response of the king. Yet here God has raised up a man after His own heart, a man who will faithfully shepherd Israel.

David, who will succeed Saul as king. David, who speaks of "his lord" in Psalm 110.

Is it any wonder that we come back to Bethlehem so often at Christmastime? We find ourselves in Samuel's predicament. We are tired and distressed. We doubt the outcomes of the future. We fear for what will come to our nation and our descendants.

God sends us right back to the source. We may go with fear and meet others who fear as well. We may not even know what it is we are afraid of! He knows, though, that the answer to our fears is not a light and fluffy hug but a new way of life. Whether it is for Samuel, sent to a anoint the new king, or for us, sent to the newborn King to find new life, God has a plan.

And a return to Bethlehem is a great place to start.

Where is your Bethlehem? Where did you first find your hope in God? What do you need to bring that hope back?

Hymn for the Day: "Good Christian Men Rejoice" tr. by John Mason Neale. (#183 in the *2008 Baptist Hymnal* from Lifeway Worship.)

Day 5: Up on Mt. Moriah

"Abraham called the name of that place The LORD Will Provide, as it is said to this day, "In the mount of the LORD it will be provided."" (Genesis 22:14 NASB)

Mt. Moriah. It was a place some distance from where Abraham lived. Based on the text of Genesis, it was a three day journey from the tents of home with Sarah. Abraham and Isaac made that journey with two of the family's servants. They had little choice, for God had commanded a sacrifice.

A sacrifice unlike any that Abraham had ever contemplated. God had spoken, though, and commanded that Abraham take his son, his only son, Isaac, and sacrifice him. Sacrifice the son he loved, the son he had waited on for decades. That son, the heir to the promises of God, was to be killed in the name of worship.

It sounds abhorrent, and we see in God's law given later that God saw it as abhorrent, too (Deuteronomy 18:10). Abraham has no book of Deuteronomy to consult. He has only his faith that God knows best, and he has learned not to ignore the commands of the Lord. Therefore, he sets out. On the third day, he lifts up his eyes and sees the place God has commanded. Abraham begins the assent to do what he never thought would happen.

We find ourselves in similar times. I truly hope you have never climbed a mountain intent on sacrificing a living human being, but we look at this as an analogy. Abraham on Mt. Moriah faces a sacrifice he never thought of making.

What sacrifice do we face?

Perhaps it is a career that is no longer compatible with your integrity. You lift up your eyes and see your bills, your desires, and your family. You cannot sacrifice your responsibilities, and you cannot sacrifice your integrity either. What are you to do? Is God even involved? Does He notice?

Or worse, there is a relationship in your life that you now know stands between you and God. It is not one that you cannot abandon, like caring for your infant and minor children, but it holds your heart tightly. Perhaps it is that you are holding on too tightly to someone you must let go, perhaps you are planning a future that has no future. You look up and see the loneliness. That is it.

Yet, in faith, you start up the mountain. You leave behind those who would stop you, and you make the climb.

Just as Abraham did on Moriah.

And you find what he found: God provided a sacrifice suitable to Him. For Abraham, it was a ram in a thicket. That ram foreshadowed the coming Son of God who died for us all, the suitable sacrifice for our lives.

For you, God provides. He does not always provide

what you expect. You will still have to make hard decisions. But He is able to provide for your needs while you keep faith with your word. He will soothe your loneliness and your broken heart if you will come to Him. There is no sacrifice He asks that He Himself has not experienced.

We see it on Moriah, and we see it in our lives today.

Do you ever think God does not understand your troubles? Are you facing an obstacle too great? Is there someone out there that you can be the hand of the Lord to provide for?

Hymn for the Day: "Holy, Holy, Holy" by Reginald Heber. (#68 in the *2008 Baptist Hymnal* from Lifeway Worship.)

Week 3

Sunday: In the Heart of the House of God

And an angel of the Lord appeared to him, standing to the right of the altar of incense. (Luke 1:11 NASB)

We go about life and rarely stop to consider the grand narrative of history that exists around us. Rather like Sam and Frodo, we remember the great stories of prior generations but do not recognize that we live in the midst of a story of our own. Our life may seem like a footnote or a bit part, but until the whole story is written who can see where the plot hinged? Only the author.

With this thought in mind, we come to the heart of the house of God, the temple in Jerusalem. Luke 1 tells us of a man named Zacharias who showed up to work as a priest one day at the temple. In the custom of the time, a random event was used to choose someone to go in and burn incense. That lot fell to Zacharias who followed the habits he had seen for years and went in to perform his duties.

He had seen this process unfold many times before. He had participated, either by being chosen or serving the one who had, for a lifetime. He knew exactly what to expect: go in, heat up the incense, spread the sweet savor around, and leave. Finish his month and go home. Routine was the expectation of Zacharias, even in the temple of the Living God.

Something else happened that day, for when he looked up in the temple, he saw an angel. Luke's detail about the angel being to the right of the altar almost sounds like the angel was in the way! Gabriel was there for a reason and it was more important than the incense.

Today as you go through your spiritual routine, consider Zacharias in the heart of the house of God. He had a role to fulfill in the grand narrative of God's work of redemption. So do you. You will not see an angel standing next to the incense today, nor will you become the father of John the Baptist.

But you will see the Word of God, if you will look. You will find something that can be utterly earth-shattering for you. You will see that the message of the Gospel has gone forth, and still goes forward. What happens in response to the Gospel?

Just what Zacharias heard that day: families are restored, the disobedient repent, and the people are ready for the Lord. You and I have the same great and joyful opportunity that was revealed to Zacharias, to proclaim the coming of Jesus.

To see it, we must be in the right place. The right place is exactly where God has commanded us to be. For Zacharias, it was the temple on his given day. For us, it is gathered with God's people when possible and being salt and light in the world when appropriate. Great things happen in the heart of the house of God, and great things happen where the people of God are obedient.

Let us not face this Christmas as routine, but let us instead look for those great things.

When is the last time you read every word of the songs you sing in church? Or listened diligently to all the message? Be aware today that the routine provides a framework to hear the Word of God.

Hymn for the day: "Angels, from the Realms of Glory" by James Montgomery (#179 in the *2008 Baptist Hymnal* by Lifeway Worship)

Special music for the week: "One Christmas Eve" by Wayne Watson, on the album *One Christmas Eve*.

Day 1: In the House of Mary

The angel said to her, "Do not be afraid, Mary; for you have found favor with God. (Luke 1:30 NASB)

Some time after his trip to the house of God, Gabriel makes another stop to deliver a message. This time, he is not in the elaborate temple. He is not in a palace or even, most likely, a wealthy home. He is in an ordinary home in a little town called Nazareth.

The home of a young lady named Mary. Mary's home, and her backstory, are part of the unknowns of Christmas. While tradition fills in a few gaps and possibilities, really all that is certain is that she was unwed but betrothed. Her home was one expecting the normal progression of life. Even among the Jews longing for a Messiah, there's not much evidence they expected Him specifically at this time.

Gabriel greeted Mary there, in her home. She was likely going about her ordinary life and doing the things which were before her as a betrothed young woman in Israel. Whole studies could be done on what all that means, and perhaps they have been. We see just a hint.

We know that Mary first felt both fear and confusion at the announcement of Gabriel. How do we know? Luke tells us she was perplexed, and Gabriel tells her not to fear. This gives us a glimpse of her state of mind, but then we see something else in her: commitment. She asked how this could happen, but then accepted an explanation that relied on faith above facts.

Mary was an ordinary girl, one who had kept the ways of God. The message of Gabriel says that she found "favor" with God, but we cannot put too much on that word. Why not? It is the word for "grace," not for anything earned. Mary found the grace of God. Her little home now houses something greater than imaginable. She had been given the grace of God, and through her Son grace would be given to the whole world.

What does the house of Mary say to us? Nothing, because it's a building that has long since gone away. It reminds us, though, of our own material belongings. While they are necessary for life, just as Mary needed a roof over her head and food in her belly, they are not enduring. The actions of obedience, the times when we say "I am the servant of the Lord, let it be as you have said," (Luke 1:38) are what endure for years to come. Thus we learn to move our focus.

Further, we learn another important truth from Mary's house. It's not there any longer. The years have not preserved it for us to visit either in museum or pilgrimage. The presence of God was there, but He is not limited to that one place. We need not fear that our location prohibits us from being found by God, nor do we need to go somewhere else to find Him. Let Him find you where you are and show His grace in you and through you.

Have you ever thought you were too far away for God to find you? Or that your circumstances were too lowly to be of use?

Hymn for the day: "How Great Our Joy" (#202 in the *2008 Baptist Hymnal* by Lifeway Worship)

Day 2: *In the House of Elizabeth*

"And how has it happened to me, that the mother of my Lord would come to me?" (Luke 1:43 NASB)

We find ourselves a fly on the wall as two women meet in a doorway. Inside, an older woman deals with a joyous burden. She is six months pregnant, and the toll on her body is showing. She is tired. It is no longer easy to rest at night, and she has long-held habits that do not involve frequent rests for the sake of a growing baby. She is Elizabeth, the wife of Zacharias.

Outside the door, we find a young woman. We know only that she has never been married and that she also expects a baby. She is not as far along as Elizabeth. Her child is promised to be a son as well, announced to her not too long ago. Her name is Mary. She will have a husband, but that has not happened yet.

What do these two talk about? They spend three months together, so they discuss many things. What we do know is that the meeting of the two features Elizabeth's baby expressing joy at the sound of Mary's voice. Mary, in response, erupts in praise. Not of Elizabeth, nor even of her own greatness, but of the Lord who has blessed her. She rejoices in God her Savior and celebrates the mercy of God.

There is one other in the house, though, beside the two women and their sons. Zacharias is likely there as well, quiet and contemplating. He knows all about John, his son, and the coming Messiah. But he cannot say much about it. He cannot say anything at all, because his doubt brought the sign of silence to him (Luke 1:20.)

Your place, today, may be like Zacharias' place in the house he shared with Elizabeth. You are dealing with the consequences of doubt or sin or disobedience. To make matters worse, you are surrounded by people exuberant with the blessings of God. They carry on, singing and praising, and you sit, alone and quiet.

Bitterness crouches at the door of your emotions, and if you invite it in it will destroy you. It is hard to resist, though, for why should any be happy if you cannot be? Zacharias could have lashed out. He could have caused much more difficulty.

Instead, I see him taking the wise path here. His mouth got him into trouble in the first place, but now he wisely uses his ears. He listens. He hears the joy of Mary and how Elizabeth shares it. He sees that not only was Gabriel right about Elizabeth, he was right about the coming Messiah.

So he sits in the house of Elizabeth, and as he does so, the truth finds him. He is the first man to hear of the coming Messiah because Jesus comes to him. Even as he deals with the consequences of his own shortcomings.

He will come to you, as well.

Are you frustrated? Are you angry? Take a few minutes to see the joy of Christmas in others, and let the Savior come to you.

Hymn for the day: "God Rest Ye Merry, Gentlemen," authorship uncertain. I would recommend Meredith Andrews' version titled "He Has Come for Us" on the album *Behold the Savior*.

Day 3: In the House of Joseph

But when he had considered this, behold, an angel of the Lord appeared to him in a dream, saying, "Joseph, son of David, do not be afraid to take Mary as your wife; for the Child who has been conceived in her is of the Holy Spirit." (Matthew 1:20 NASB)

Most cultures have a minimum amount of "family" that is necessary for survival. While the modern American minimum requires its own discussion, it is certain that the Roman Empire saw a mother and a father as the absolute minimum. How so? In certain corners of the empire, property rights were only allocated to men(though this changed through the years) and many religions had separate practices for men and women.

In Judea, and among the Jewish religion of its inhabitants, this was the case. For Mary to be safe and provided for in the world, she needed a husband. If the son of Mary was to take His place among the population, He needed a father. This was not an option, no matter how we view such systems now.

Yet who would be willing to take on this challenge? John, Elizabeth's son, has a definite father in Zacharias. Mary, though, professes to be pregnant and unwed by the action of God. One can imagine that this does not play well with potential suitors. Not that she is able to examine options, since she is betrothed to a man named Joseph. Joseph, who is going to be accused of not controlling himself when Mary has a baby less than nine months after the wedding.

Joseph, who knows he is not responsible, wants to separate from his commitment to Mary. He would like to protect her by not demanding her execution, but he wants to protect himself by moving on. Mary's story is not really believable, anyway, and this will allow her to marry whomever is the father of this baby.

Then an angel comes. Matthew records the visit and apparently has no concern for the angel's name. What we do know is that Joseph accepts the challenge. He takes Mary as his bride, refrains from consummating the marriage until after the birth of Jesus, and provides the home Jesus needs.

What do we learn from Joseph? He has no definite quotes in all of Scripture. His next mention is when Jesus turns up missing at age twelve, and then he becomes a "past tense" figure. Jesus is referred to as "the carpenter's son" as He begins preaching. Should we take Joseph to mean we must build in wood?

No, but we should see this: you may be facing the consequences of someone else's life. Whether it is their sin or their blessing that has brought the burden, they are carrying it, just as Mary carried Jesus. They need help and they have asked for yours.

You possess the opportunity to hold someone up and strengthen their hands as they serve the Lord Jesus Christ.

You sit, perhaps not as critical as Joseph, but still valuable to the lives of others. Take up the task today. You may not be remembered as well. Your words may not be recalled. But your actions will make a difference.

Who can you encourage today? Take the time to find to encourage someone else, near or far.

Hymn for the Day: "I Heard the Bells on Christmas Day" by Henry Wadsworth Longfellow (#187 in the *2008 Baptist Hymnal* from Lifeway Worship).

Day 4: In the House of the Magi

"Where is He who has been born King of the Jews? For we saw His star in the east and have come to worship Him." (Matthew 2:2 NASB)

Your life is consumed with waiting. Waiting and watching. Wondering when, or even if, something exciting will come your way. While you wait, your life is overrun with the humdrum. You give advice; you chart the advance of years; you pass on the wisdom of the ages. Mainly, though, you wait and watch for something different.

Then one night things change. A sign, a miraculous moment, an anomaly in life bursts through. It is beyond your wildest expectations, and it causes you to abandon your life of waiting. No longer do you dispense advice or watch the skies. You load up and set out, having seen what you had heard for years was coming. You follow the best of instructions.

And come out in the wrong place, causing problems you never imagined.

Still, you go down in history as the "Wise Men" of the Christmas story. Shall we back up and examine how this is their story?

The Magi were a class of astronomers/philosophers in Persia. They had been around for centuries, entering the Bible story in the book of Daniel when the Medo-Persian Empire conquered Babylon. As the events shifted back to Israel, the Magi faded from view, but history reminds us they were still there.

And they continue to watch the stars. Then one night a group of Magi see something in the heavens that tells them the King of the Jews has been born. Many times I have seen attempts to define what they saw, but it is outside the scope of astronomy to give us a clear answer. It may have been a rightly timed natural phenomenon, for the heavens declare the glory of God (Psalm 19:1). It may have been supernatural.

Whatever the sign, it is enough for these men to load up and travel across the wilderness to Jerusalem. They pass from one kingdom to another and come to the capital of the Jews. At this point, their travel breaks down. Having asked for directions, they stir up the reigning king of the Jews, Herod. This, in turn, stirs up everyone in town, for Herod is not one to be crossed lightly.

The Magi receive directions, though, and make their way to Bethlehem. The directions are found in Micah, a book written quite a few centuries before their journey. If only they had known, back in the house of the Magi, they could have made the straight trip.

This reminds us of an important truth. There is wisdom available to us, already written and in the Word of God. Unlike the Magi, we are not wading through countless scrolls from foreign lands. We have the text right there in front of us and have precious little excuse for not considering what God has already said.

Perhaps you, like the Magi, have taken off in haste without fully considering what God says about your journey or your destination. There is no time like now to stop and look at the Word. See where you are going.

Because when you reach where God tells you to go, you will be overjoyed. Just like the Magi were (Matthew 2:10).

Where do you turn for guidance? Do you ask all the sources? Do you follow signs? Or do you seek the Word of God?

Hymn for the Day: "It Came Upon the Midnight Clear" by Edmund H. Sears. (#188 in the *2008 Baptist Hymnal* from Lifeway Worship.)

Day 5: In the Courts of the House of God

And there was a man in Jerusalem whose name was Simeon; and this man was righteous and devout, looking for the consolation of Israel; and the Holy Spirit was upon him.(Luke 2:25 NASB)

And there was a prophetess, Anna the daughter of Phanuel, of the tribe of Asher. She was advanced in years and had lived with her husband seven years after her marriage, and then as a widow to the age of eighty-four. She never left the temple, serving night and day with fastings and prayers.(Luke 2:36–37 NASB)

Today we come back to the very same temple where Zacharias had his vision. This time, though, we are not deep inside. Nor are we over by the altar of incense. Instead, we are out in the outer courts. Public access to the temple was, generally speaking, divided among three areas. The outermost area was the limit for the Gentiles. Closer in was an area where Jewish women were permitted to enter. Closest in to the actions and work of the priests was an area reserved for observant, Jewish men.

A great deal of everyday life went on in Jerusalem as people passed through these areas. Some people spent more time there than others, as the temple precincts were open for prayer. Provided, of course, they stayed where they belonged. This was the way it had always been, a long-standing tradition that enforced a division among the people who desired to draw near to God.

It does give us some context for events that occurred in the temple. If a woman was involved, it could not have happened any further in than the court of women. Likewise, a Gentile's presence tells us that the greatest distance is in view, as far away from the Holy of Holies as one could get while still being "in the Temple."

These courts are our location for the day. Let us sneak inward from the court of the Gentiles and take a quick look before we are roundly tossed out on our ears. We may find some interesting people.

First, as we enter the court of women, we see a woman. Anna is her name. She is quite old, having lived not only fourscore years, but four more. She has a space here, though, and it appears that she pretty well stays in the temple. What does she do? She fasts, she prays, and she speaks the words of God.

But mostly, she seems to be waiting.

Quickly, let us duck behind this crowd and enter the court of Israel, where only observant Jewish men are permitted. Tighten that shawl up, you in the back! You'll get us in trouble! This is the only way to see what's next.

It is not so much what's next as who. There's another older person here, this one a man. He, like Anna, spends his time in prayer and service. Perhaps he aids those who are overwhelmed by the ceremony and circumstance here. It is hard to see what he does, much like her. If we were writing a romantic film, they would find each other on a rare trip outside and live happily ever after.

For now, though, he appears to be waiting. Like her, waiting. Hear his voice? He calls out that the consolation of Israel is coming. That someday one will come to bind up the broken-hearted and proclaim good news to the poor. Hear him?

Wait, is that a guard? We better clear out, and quickly.

Are you waiting for something? Do you see opportunities to serve in the meantime?

Hymn for the Day: "While Shepherds Watch Their Flocks" by Nahum Tate. (#203 in the *2008 Baptist Hymnal from Lifeway Worship.*)

Week 4

Sunday: By the Waters of Babylon

"By the rivers of Babylon, there we sat down and wept, when we remembered Zion." (Psalm 137:1 NASB)

We need to make one more circle around history on our way to Bethlehem. Our first stop is by the rivers of Babylon. Here we see many a sad face as the people sit and weep. Who are they and why are they weeping?

They are the exiles of Jerusalem, taken in captivity when the nation of Judah fell. They weep for their loved ones who fell in battle. They weep for their homes. They weep for the temple. They weep for the loss of all they have known. Life has changed irrevocably.

Many factors built up to cause the fall of Jerusalem. There was blame for the previous generations. There was blame for the government. Blame for the religious leaders. Truthfully, though, the blame belonged to the people in total. There had been problems but they had profits. So, there was less willingness to deal with them. And society crumbled because of it.

You may be sitting by your own river of Babylon. How you got here is part of your story, one that you know all too well. You may have just barely known what was happening before you turned up here. You may be able to map it all out perfectly. Your "could have" and "should have" list is longer than your Christmas shopping list.

Making it worse, you knew it all along. Like the people of Judah, you had the Word of God in hand. You had people trying to teach and influence you to do what that Word said. Or worse, you were brought to this desolate river because someone else failed to honor what they knew was right!

Either way, the situation is bleak. At least, it is bleak to you. The world sees it as Christmas time. A time when anyone not named Scrooge should be happy! Sing!

Celebrate! You just don't have it in you right now. Your harp is hung up, and there is nothing to celebrate.

Like the people of Judah, you would sing if you had hope but hope has left you. What can you do?

Look back at the manger. The same people, the same families, who hung their harps in the willows came to the manger. It is here that hope comes from, not from our own circumstances. The Israelites by the river thought all was lost if they forgot the past, but the hope they needed was still in the future. Our hope has come and soon we reach the day when we remember His birth.

Find hope again this year. You may not find enough yet to sing the songs this year. You may still feel like you are in that foreign land where life has dragged you. Nourish that spark and let it grow; let it start at the manger and catch fire throughout your days.

What is sapping joy from your life? Do you feel

pulled away from God? Are there others you can gather with to help strengthen you?

Hymn for the day: "Praise to the Lord, the Almighty" by Joachim Neander, translated by Catherine Winkworth (#1 in the *2008 Baptist Hymnal* by Lifeway Worship)

Special music for the week: Find a copy of Handel's Messiah. If you cannot listen to the whole thing, which can be hard at one sitting if you are not watching it live, then focus on these two segments: "For Unto Us a Child is Born" and the Hallelujah Chorus.

Day 1: Out in Samaria

The king of Assyria brought men from Babylon and from Cuthah and from Avva and from Hamath and Sephar-vaim, and settled them in the cities of Samaria in place of the sons of Israel. So they possessed Samaria and lived in its cities. (2 Kings 17:24 NASB)

Behold, the land of Israel! Now occupied by people from all over the place, as you can see above. This is not the plan that the people expected. The Israelites had come to the land and expected to stay there, but they did not keep the covenant God gave them. After generations of sin and rejection, the Lord brought judgment and took the people from the land. Then the Assyrians moved new people onto the land.

That saga is an interesting one and has spawned many an historic hunt for the Israelite tribes that were deported. Turn your eyes to the people who came in. Many of these families became established in the land and never left. They formed a district under the Assyrians, which later came under the Neo-Babylonians and Persians, around the city of Samaria. The result? They came to be known as Samaritans.

The Samaritans were the descendants of this mixed multitude moved into the land by Assyria. They intermarried with each other and with surviving Israelites. Out of this evolved a syncretistic religion, one that merged the religious beliefs of the various cultures.

Samaria became the Old Testament image of a great cultural melting pot. Religion came to look like a buffet: take a little of this, a little of that, and have what you like. The echoes of Samaria are heard in many modern cultures. We are often given the idea that religious beliefs should be changed as the winds change.

Yet this same Samaria is visited in the wake of Christmas. We do not see anyone labeled a Samaritan at the manger, but we do see Samaritans in the life of Jesus. The most notable one is a Samaritan woman who is the key figure of John 4. She meets Jesus at the well of the city of Sychar.

He speaks with her about worship and life, highlighting that the Samaritans worship without knowing. Then He tells her that the Truth she needs to know is right there, talking to her. She knows that the Samaritans have been looking for a Messiah. Now He is here.

God works by doing things many of us would not expect. His plans are never thwarted. The Israelites had been commanded to shine a light for the Gentiles, but it never quite happened. Instead, God brought the Gentiles into Israel. Then He came in the flesh; Immanuel not just for the Jews but for Samaritans and Gentiles as well.

This is the great news of Christmas. No matter how muddled our heritage, no matter what our faith was like before Jesus came, we can worship what we know. Not only "what" we know, but who. And that is so much greater.

Are there people near you who are not like you? Can you find out how to share the love of Jesus with people not like you? Either by joining in worship or going out to serve, try to extend your view of the people of God beyond the mirror.

Hymn for the day: "Hark! The Herald Angels Sing" by Charles Wesley and George Whitfield, (#192 in the *2008 Baptist Hymnal* by Lifeway Worship)

Day 2: *Near the Gates of Jerusalem*

Now in those days a decree went out from Caesar

Augustus, that a census be taken of all the inhabited earth.

(Luke 2:1 NASB)

Caesar Augustus was the first official Roman

Emperor. Yet his orders affected the people of Israel such as

Mary and Joseph, driving them to Bethlehem. Why? Our

journey to the manger makes a brief stop at the gates of

Jerusalem in 63 BC. During this time, the Hasmonean

Kingdom of Israel was a small but independent nation. Then

chaos came in a succession crisis, and the Roman Empire

got involved.

While not directly relevant to Christmas, I would

make this immediate point: never get the Roman Empire

involved. They will take over, not help. You might not have

experienced this, but it is exactly what occurred in Jerusalem

that year. It happened again a few decades later, putting

Herod the Great on the throne.

There are two major effects from this. The first is the return of the people of Israel to being a conquered nation instead of an independent one. This brings their messianic hopes back to the forefront.

It's not unlike how many of us are: when things go well, our spiritual commitments run a little shallow. If there is no need in our faces, we falter from our drive to draw near to God.

Let things go poorly, though, and we run quickly to faith. Even if our beliefs have not been important for years, we run to their shelter when times are tough.

The promises of God, though, are not only for the foul weather days. He had promised the people of Israel the Messiah. He had promised David that someone would sit on his throne forever. While it took the Romans to get the Israelites looking strongly for the fulfillment of these promises, the Lord of the promises had never slacked in His work.

The second effect is more easily felt. If Israel had remained an independent nation on the borders of Rome, then Augustus Caesar would have held no authority over the region. Then, when he ordered a tax count, his administrators in the region would have no reason to order Mary and Joseph back to Bethlehem.

Yet God had already said they would go back to Bethlehem, for His prophet Micah said that the Messiah would be born there. The Roman domination, for all that was disliked, was critical. It became even more critical some three decades after the manger, when Pontius Pilate washed his hands and sent Jesus to the cross. From that cross, He made atonement for our sins. From that cross, He went into a borrowed tomb, where He did not stay but rose again.

All the chaos of our life, both of our own making and the making of others, works together for the purposes of God (Romans 8:28). It is not always good, nor is always pleasant. Yet God has worked all of this together that you and I may know Him and draw near. Come to the manger, and know Him better. In the end, He is the one who makes sense of it all.

Are you weary of the circumstances of life? Can you look back and see one way God has used negative things to draw you to Him? Can you find a way to encourage someone else in a difficult time this week?

Hymn for the day: "Angels We Have Heard on High" (#184 in the *2008 Baptist Hymnal* by Lifeway Worship)

Day 3: *Amidst the Desolation of the Land*

"For a child will be born to us, a son will be given to us; and the government will rest on His shoulders; and His name will be called Wonderful Counselor, Mighty God, Eternal Father, Prince of Peace. There will be no end to the increase of His government or of peace, on the throne of David and over his kingdom, to establish it and to uphold it with justice and righteousness from then on and forevermore. The zeal of the LORD of hosts will accomplish this." (Isaiah 9:6–7 NASB)

Earlier we took a look at Israel in captivity, sitting by the rivers of Babylon. Today, we return to the land of Israel. It is a dark and desolate place right now. War has swept the land, and the majority of the Israelites have been deported by the Assyrians. The southern kingdom, called Judah, still stands. Centered on Jerusalem, this kingdom feels the inevitability of its fall. Isaiah is God's prophet of the time, called to comfort and correct the people.

We find him today in the midst of the desolation. Earlier we read of Isaiah's encounter with King Ahaz, and today we find him writing the words of the Lord. The exact time and place of his writing is uncertain. He writes of gloom and anguish and of greater gloom to come. It is a desolate time, for the land and for the people.

We find ourselves in the midst of our own desolation. There is desolation in the land as years of economic turmoil continue to take their toll. There is desolation in our families as feuds simmer and boil over. Desolation in our government as factionalism has replaced cooperation. While Judah saw desolation coming from the outside, many of us live in lands that see desolation rising up within, brought on by the sinfulness of people.

We may even find that desolation in our personal lives. In some cases, forced from the outside. In others, built up from within. The resulting desolation remains the same, though. We cry out for help...or we shut down and attempt to live in self-sufficiency.

Isaiah stands surrounded by the desolation, and his words echo into our own lives. The desolation will not last forever! Indeed, One is coming who will rebuild the desolation. One is coming who will never lose the throne or the power. He will be established in righteousness and justice forevermore.

When He comes, He will be the Counselor that we need, guiding and directing. He will be the Father who lasts forever, never abandoning His children and never dying. He will be the prince who rules in peace, not seeking conflict but answering it with righteousness that cannot be denied.

He will be, in all things, Wonderful.

The desolation may surround you today. You may look at this description of who God is, seeing that His zeal and His passion will accomplish this without any need for help, and think "that will be nice when it happens!"

It already has. That is why come to the manger. For this is the child born to us, the Son given to us. Jesus. Prince of Peace, Immanuel.

Who can you make peace with this Christmas? What relationships can you restore? Will you take a first step of sharing a moment this year?

Hymn for the day: "The First Noel" (#180 in the *2008 Baptist Hymnal* by Lifeway Worship)

Day 4: Back in Bethlehem (for Christmas Eve)

And while they were there, the time came for her to give birth. And she gave birth to her firstborn son and wrapped him in swaddling cloths and laid him in a manger, because there was no place for them in the inn. (Luke 2:6–7 ESV)

Finally, we are back to the manger. We come back, as we do every year, and remind ourselves of what happened. How on that one night so long ago, a new mother gave birth. How in a world that had no room, the Savior of mankind was born. How we would not have understood or known God had Jesus not come to make Him plain (John 1).

We come back. Even as the challenges we face on a year to year basis are different, we come back. There is something comforting in the tradition. In it we find a reminder that, though life changes, God remains faithful. A reminder that His promises are sure.

We find a reminder that what we believe is rooted in a historical event. Christmas may not have happened on December 25th. It certainly did not happen in the year "0" and cause the turning of the calendar. That was a later adjustment to the counting of years. But it happened nonetheless. We can remember the day without being particular about the date.

We benefit by coming back. All of the advanced theology in the world does us no good if we lose the truth of the manger. Even if we could express all the proper nuance of the Incarnation, it would matter not at all if we did not know the Jesus we speak of!

Why? Because this is love, that Jesus put on flesh, dwelt among us, and gave His life as the ransom for many. Love was shown at Christmas, not merely because Jesus came in the flesh, but because of the cross He was headed to from day one.

As we come back to the manger, we are reminded that

the foundation of all our faith is this real event, this real action of love shown by God. We may dislike what God has said at times, but we cannot look in the face of God as He is in the manger and deny that He came for us. We cannot look at the face of God on the cross and deny His love for us.

His faithfulness is real. It is the stable constant of our world. Whatever you have happening in your world right now, take a few moments and be grateful for that stable constant. It is where our peace and hope come from.

If you have never come near to God, if you are wondering where to find Him again, or if you are simply seeking a way to express your devotion, may I suggest we start in the same place this year? Start at the manger, where we know He was.

Let us grow together in faith as we remember that night again this year.

Can you find a minute or two of peace and calm

today? Seek it out and take that time to remember that moment when Christ came for us. Take comfort in the repetition, because it reminds us that some things never change.

Hymn for the day: "Silent Night, Holy Night" by Joseph Mohr, translated by John Freeman Young (#206 in the *2008 Baptist Hymnal* by Lifeway Worship). I particularly like the version recorded by Lady Antebellum on *On This Winter's Night.*

Day 5: In the Fields and the Heavens (for Christmas Day)

And an angel of the Lord appeared to them, and the glory of the Lord shone around them, and they were filled with great fear. And the angel said to them, "Fear not, for behold, I bring you good news of great joy that will be for all the people. For unto you is born this day in the city of David a Savior, who is Christ the Lord." (Luke 2:9–11 ESV)

Christmas Day. The sun has risen, and life begins. It may be a busy day on the calendar. It may be a simple one. You may have to work today. We cannot always choose our days, can we?

There were some who had to work the first Christmas as well. They were shepherds, abiding with their flocks. After all, if something came around with an eye for lamb, it had to be stopped. So the shepherds were there, on duty with the sheep. They were unaware of the glory of God that was revealed not too far away.

The shepherds had their duty to fulfill that day, so they were with the sheep. Unlike the Magi, or Mary and Joseph, or John and Elizabeth, or Simeon and Anna, these men had no warnings of what was coming. It is easy to overlook people like the shepherds. They are just there, background people for daily life.

God does not overlook them, just as He did not overlook the shepherds.

In fact, it was important enough that He sent angels to bring the shepherds into the story. Are these the same angels that contacted the major characters in the story? Is Gabriel among them? We cannot say for certain, but we know this: the testimony of Scripture never has angels doing minor tasks. Never.

Bringing the shepherds into the story was important.

Today, you may be the shepherds in the Christmas story. You stand on the outskirts. Your time is busy with the daily events of life. You have a duty to perform. God has not forgotten you, though, and when He proclaims "peace on earth," it is sent to you. Peace in the fields, even as you work.

Perhaps you are not busy about the business of the day. If that is your blessing today, I give you this challenge: God sent angels that first Christmas. Rather than sitting around thinking about how much better off you are than those poor shepherds out in the field, be the messenger of good news that God sends. Go forth to praise God and make known the wonders that are in the manger.

Do be careful to not be annoying: that guy working the movie theater counter may just want to go home! But carry the message of Christmas with you throughout the day, and all the days that follow. Whether you are at work in the fields today or return to them later, carry with you the light of hope: Glory to God in the Highest! For a child has been born to us, and He is Christ, our Lord.

Who do you know that needs to be encouraged? How can you take the peace God gives to all the places you will go between now and next Christmas?

Hymn for the day: "O Holy Night" by John S. Dwight (#194 in the *2008 Baptist Hymnal* by Lifeway Worship)

Wrapping Up: The Twelve Days of Christmas

We have come through the four weeks leading up to Christmas, but it's not over yet! You may be familiar with the third most annoying Christmas song in history, "The Twelve Days of Christmas." (The other two? Ask me via email, but one involves the most deadly non-human mammal in Africa.) What are the "Twelve Days of Christmas?" They are not merely an excuse to give odd gifts. Instead, these are the days that fall between Christmas and Epiphany, the date traditionally attributed to the visit of the Magi.

An in-depth history of why those days are, and are not, celebrated by all is beyond the scope here. I do want to encourage you to keep your habit of a daily devotional going, though, so I want to give you some prompts for each of the next twelve days. I'll give a Scripture references and some brief thoughts.

Before we go on, let me suggest not cutting off the Christmas soundtrack for the next twelve days. You can go back to the introduction to see some recommended Christmas albums. Music is a great part of celebrating Christmas.

Day 1: The Palace of Herod (Matthew 2:1-12)

As you look at the story of the Magi and Herod, think about this: how far would you go to protect your position in life? We readily (and rightly!) condemn Herod's actions. Yet how often we are willing to sacrifice others for our own sake? Further, our own selfishness drives others away from us. Note that the Magi are unable to return to Jerusalem with good news. Instead, they return home without sharing their exceedingly great joy.

Day 2: Temple with Anna (Luke 2:36-38)

We looked at Anna earlier. We saw her waiting. Now we see her waiting finished. She has seen the Messiah. She goes from seeing the infant Jesus to telling all who will listen about Him. What do we do after Christmas? Certainly we should speak of the good times we had, of the gifts and the family, but let us not forget the manger and who we have celebrated!

Day 3: Temple with Simeon (Luke 2:25-35)

As with Anna, we looked at Simeon earlier. He is also released from his waiting. His hope was that he would see the Lord's Messiah before his death. Now he has seen Jesus. His prayer? Not that he would get more years, but praise that God will dismiss him in peace. How are you greeting the passing time? Do you hold tightly to years that will never be recovered? Or are you ready for God to send you to the next step in peace?

Day 4: Egypt (Matthew 2:13-15)

Matthew tends to take Old Testament passages and apply them in ways we would not imagine. For example, he finds the flight of Joseph, Mary, and Jesus to Egypt as the fulfillment of Hosea 11:1. Most of Hosea's readers saw that verse as referring to the Exodus. Who would be right? Both. The Exodus was a unique event and Matthew connects God's deliverance of the people there with God's deliverance in Jesus. Joseph, Mary, and Jesus escape Herod by fleeing to another corner of the Roman Empire. It is very likely that the gifts of the Magi are used up here, especially the gold.

Day 5: Nazareth (Matthew 2:20-23; Luke 2:39-40)

Now we find the Holy Family (Joseph, Mary, and Jesus) in Nazareth. Putting the texts together, it looks like they thought about returning to Bethlehem instead of Nazareth, but Herod's family cannot be trusted. Therefore they go to Galilee, and here Jesus grows up. As He grows, God's grace is upon Him and people come to know Him as a wise young man. His true parentage is not well-known and the people see Him grow like any other young man. Likely only Joseph and Mary know this, for we see the people of Nazareth think of Him merely as Joseph's son in Luke 4.

Day 6: Baptism in the Jordan (Mark 1:9-13)

Jesus has left home at this point. He comes to His cousin John at the Jordan River and is baptized. Here we see something rare in Scripture: the Trinity of God revealed as plainly as possible. Christians believe that God exists as "Trinity," meaning three distinct persons who are still unified. Whole books exist to explain this idea, but we see it here in the Jordan. Jesus is in the water, being baptized. The Holy Spirit is seen descending like a dove, and the voice of the Father comes from Heaven. God is one, yet we see Him as three here. Further, this kicks off the public ministry of Jesus. He goes out to face temptation and comes back to die for our sins.

Day 7: Golgotha (John 19:16-30)

Christmas means very little without the cross. Jesus did not come so that we could remember Him as a cute baby. He came to die in our place. This comes to its fullness at Golgotha, the Place of the Skull. When Jesus proclaims that "it is finished" in verse 30, He means more than just His earthly life. His mission, His purpose in the Incarnation, is finished. Sin is defeated, death is broken, and redemption is here.

Day 8: The Garden (Matthew 28)

Death is not the end. Not for Jesus, and not for those who follow Him. Instead, we find Him alive and in the Garden of Gethsemane three days after the cross. He is risen, just as He said. The Word of the Lord cannot be broken, not even by death. This is true love: that Jesus died for us and yet is risen. Our sins can be forgiven. Let us take the message of the Risen Lord Jesus to the world!

Day 9: The Execution of Stephen (Acts 7)

Where is Jesus in this story? Standing at the right hand of God as His servant Stephen is executed. We are called to take the Word to the world, to carry the message of the Risen Lord. The world does not always want to hear it. That may mean trouble for us. Sometimes, Jesus will rescue us from trouble. Sometimes, though, that rescue is our reception into eternity. Faithfulness to the Lord is our purpose; avoiding trouble is not. God will determine success, and the image in Acts is of a sovereign ruler greeting a successful emissary.

Day 10: Mars Hill/Paul (Acts 17)

There is a world out there which has never heard of Jesus. At the least, they have not heard the message clearly. They may have seen some versions of Jesus, but nothing like who He truly is, as He is revealed in Scripture. What do we do? We borrow from Paul's example and find people where they are. We engage their arguments and show how everything points back to Jesus.

Day 11: Revelation (Revelation 12)

Here is the strangest part of Christmas. John sees a dragon, Satan, trying to attack Israel. Next he tries to attack Mary while she is pregnant; then he attempts to sweep away Mary and Jesus. This reminds us that there is more to life than what we see. While Scripture never commands us to focus on the supernatural matters we do not see, these events still exist. There remain unseen matters, and it was not merely the Roman Empire that Jesus dealt with in His time on Earth. It took the will of God to bring the Incarnation to pass. Nothing, not even all the powers of evil, could prevent God from redeeming His people.

Day 12: The World: The Visit of the Magi (Matthew 2:11)

The Magi come, and they bring gifts. These three gifts were the focus of my first Advent writing and are the focus of many songs and sermons this time of year. We are reminded that these wise men brought gold, frankincense, and myrrh. All of these have both symbolic and practical values. It is hard to say that the Magi knew Jesus would be king, priest, and sacrifice. There is little evidence of who they were looking for, besides the "born king of the Jews." Yet we see their gifts were brought with wisdom. What do we bring? There is nothing left for us to bring but ourselves, as the song says: "What can I give Him? I will give Him my heart."

As long as we see our heart as all of us, our entire being, will, and devotion, that's a great place to start.

About the Author

Doug Hibbard is a husband, father, and pastor. His feet have roamed through the years, but now the Grand Prairie of Arkansas is home. Besides preaching and serving the church, he writes at www.doughibbard.com and for the Home Educating Family Association at www.hedua.com

Stop by and take a look!

Made in the USA
Lexington, KY
14 November 2014